Conor Kerr

An Explosion of Feathers

Copyright © 2021 by Conor Kerr

All rights reserved. No part of this publication may be reproduced or transmitted in any form or by any means, electronic or mechanical, including photocopying, recording or any information storage and retrieval, without the written permission of the publisher. Names, characters, places and incidents are either the product of the author's imagination or used fictitiously, and any resemblance to actual persons living or dead, events or locales is entirely coincidental. All trademarks are properties of their respective owners.

Published by
BookLand Press Inc.
15 Allstate Parkway
Suite 600
Markham, Ontario L3R 5B4
www.booklandpress.com

Printed in Canada

Library and Archives Canada Cataloguing in Publication

Title: An explosion of feathers / Conor Kerr.
Names: Kerr, Conor, author.
Description: Series statement: Modern Indigenous voices
Identifiers: Canadiana (print) 20210164484 | Canadiana (ebook) 20210164492 | ISBN 9781772311532 (softcover) | ISBN 9781772311549 (EPUB)
Subjects: LCGFT: Poetry.
Classification: LCC PS8621.E7636 E97 2021 | DDC C811/.6—dc23

We acknowledge the support of the Government of Canada through the Canada Book Fund and the support of the Ontario Arts Council, an agency of the Government of Ontario. We also acknowledge the support of the Canada Council for the Arts.

For Pat

Table of Contents

faamii

Amiskwaciwâskahikan (Beaver Hills House) | 9

Cousin | 10

Lockdown | 12

Grandfather | 13

Party on the Prairies, Part I | 15

Party on the Prairies, Part II | 17

The Connor McDavid of Saskatoon Berries | 19

voyage

Toronto, Part I | 23

Toronto, Part II | 25

Loonie | 27

Cry Havoc and Paint Blue the Crack of Night | 29

I Dream of Bomb Ass Rivers (North Saskatchewan) | 31

Infinite Lek | 32

What Kind of Name is Hat for a Lake | 33

Elephants | 34

Light the Bridge | 35

Abandoned Southside | 36

A Brief History of My Childhood Injuries | 38

Eating Macaroni Soup | 39

Directions to the Culture Grounds | 40

Maverick | 43

House Fire | 44

TRC Combo | 45

Sweetgrass Dreams | 46

Fiddle Me Home | 47

The Common | 48

la keu di renn

It's All Magpies | 51

A Magpie/Métis Boy Visits Tkaronto | 53

A Magpie/Métis Boy Visits A&W | 54

A Magpie/Métis Boy Finds Some Moose Bones | 55

A Magpie/Métis Boy Attends Ukrainian Christmas | 56

A Magpie/Métis Boy Fights a Blue Jay | 57

A Magpie/Métis Boy Watches Some Cranes | 58

A Magpie/Métis Boy Goes Golfing | 60

A Magpie/Métis Boy Gets a Government Job | 61

A Magpie/Métis Boy Goes Out on the Trapline | 62

faamii

Amiskwaciwâskahikan (Beaver Hills House)

She's moonshining again. It's the holiday season
though it could be any season, and granny's
busy batching it up in the closet of her assisted living
apartment in Castledowns, North Edmonton.

We're going to swish it up
Crabapple bounce,
Dandelion wine,
Potato Champagne.

Ingredients courtesy of house gardens on Beaumaris lake
that granny reconciles with at night for the berries and flowers.
An 88 year old Métis lady, trespassing on the northside.
Parfleche replaced by a 5 cent plastic Sobey's bag.
The bush of her youth replaced by 70's suburban homes.

When the nurses go into granny's apartment they ignore
    the closet
She despairingly smiles and lets them stick their
    thermometer here
hands there. Pretty catholic those nurses, never touching
    her shine.
Bounce is too much, but hell bounce is too much
    for everyone.

Cousin

My cousin brought a mandolin on a two week canoe trip
Only learned half of the chords and words to
Copperhead Road
And didn't bother to print the rest out
No cell service
Alone on the rivers of Northern Saskatchewan
Just paddling with the loons
Eating 8 pound test walleye
Green head jigs with purple tails.
Well my name's John Lee Pettam Moore
Same as my daddies and his daddies before...
Over and over and over again

My cousin can't swim
Goes on big water canoe trips
Smokes bombers, chops wood
Master of Fine Arts in clearing a campsite
Which is a lot harder to do than it sounds
In the north when the bush slides into the
Water with all the finesse of the subtlest
Tinder swipe

My cousin climbs power poles
Plays guitar better than the mandolin
Wrestles with St. Bernards and Malamutes
Writes ACID trip journals
Can't travel to the states
Bought a pair of white jeans and wore them for a year
Straight up
Buys individual strain weeds that have some sort of fruit

In the name.
Green Apple Kush
Mango Mayhem
Pineapple Knockout
Smokes each once,
Then mixes them all together and calls it "fruit punch"

Lockdown

I called up Granny the other day,
To see how she was doing out on the island
In her locked down assisted living building.
"It's a fucking goddamn prison," she said.
"But I'm getting rich."
Granny never one to shy away from the opportunity
For a party, always has a batch of home brew going
In her closet.

Turns out since Corona Virus lockdown won't let
The residents leave and only essential staff can enter.
All the other oldies are bored as fuck and want to
Get ripped up on hooch (her words not mine).

So she's quadrupled up her batches. My father throws
The ingredients she needs up onto her second floor balcony.
And she gets it bubbling up, batch after batch,
Blackberrry Bounce.

She bottles it in anything she can find.
Old Clamato jugs,
Rinsed out milk cartons,
Tupperware,
Empty pop cans.
And sells it to the other "jailbirds."

She's planning on busting out come September if they don't
Lift the restrictions. But the money's pretty good right now,
So she'll ride it out for a bit.

Grandfather

My grandfather's songs were written in potato champagne and all night Saskatchewan Rummy games. There was none of this superimposed tradish Métis shit that you read about. No one wore a sash, half the family was "French," the other half were too Métis to be anything but an Indian. Because back then there was no delineation between who was who when the mooniyaw came a knocking.

We didn't pray to Louis Riel to rise up from his grave to save us. Our survival was written in the low paying army jobs that kept our family housed and somewhat fed. Though my grandfather preferred military jail to work. The card games were better in jail he always said. And he told me about getting released, but having a good luck streak running in the poker game so he walked down to his Lieutenant's house and broke the window so he'd get tossed back in. Get his seat back at the table you know.

My grandfather, dementia bound, dreamt of the grain elevators of Arcola, Saskatchewan and the deer that wandered the fields outside the windows of his childhood shack. He loved dogs and horses and hated anyone who told him what to do. Before he passed, he woke up one morning and dreamt that I brought him a moose steak, so a couple boys from Enoch and I went and got a moose and he got his steak.

I dream of fishing with him. Riding shotgun across the prairie. Sitt'ing on the ice and getting to reel in the lines that have fish on them. Eating venison garlic sausage and on payday thick slices of bologna wrapped in cheese. Later that night frying up the pickerel and perch from Buffalo Pound and canning the pike. I still have his "little chief" smoker.

A grade four teacher told me that there were only four kinds of Indians in Canada, coast Indians, plains Indians, woods Indians, and Eskimos. Ironic because the classroom was filled with Saulteaux, Anishnaabe, Nehiyawak, Métis and Sioux kids. I guess we were Plains?

My grandfather would lay out on the ice in an old army one piece snowsuit he stole from the base. A canvas tarp would be draped over his head so he could see down the hole to look for Wabamum Whitefish. When one swam by he would lower in his snare, made from rabbit wire attached to the end of a hockey stick to pull the fish back up.

My grandfather, young again, forty years before an open heart surgery, poached his way across the southern prairie to feed his children and his friend's families. Wild game was the difference between a long hungry life and a full one. His brother Bob, straight out of Korea would snap bullets with military precision at passing signs as they drove the back haunted hills south of Moose Jaw.

I dream of the sharptail grouse that we chased across open prairie and into caragana rows alongside abandoned settler homesteads. Waiting to see the Labrador's tails start to swing sideways and the inevitable sound of the flush before the wings breach the canopy of open sky. They're all long gone now. The homesteads, the grouse, the caragana rows, taken out for industrial farming.

We put my grandfather's ashes in an old coffee pot, stolen from the army base, that had seen thousands of rounds of cowboy coffee. Picking the grinds from your teeth, and buried it next to old hunting dogs and unmarked graves of a life long past.

Party on the Prairies, Part I

What I wouldn't give to be one
Red River Cart
over from
Pierre Falcon

As he kept the procession rolling
800 carts squeaking to 4/4 time

La Montagne Tortue ka-itohtanan,
en charette kawitapasonan,
les souliers moux kakiskenan,
l'ecorce de boulot kamisahonan

We're going to Turtle Mountain
We're going in a Red River Cart
We're going to wear moccasins
We'll wipe our asses with birch bark

You would hear us coming
From miles away
Fighting, frolicking, jigging, and singing
Cart wheels a screeching

Flanked by the finest
bison runners.
A thousand dogs barking
Between the carts

Everyone farting, and neighing, barking and braying
Then the fiddles would really start playing

We'd race the mosquito hurricanes
Mocking them until they finally caught up.
Left us floundering in mud and burning prairie
Sage in the cart circles

I would have liked to have worked with the horses
Or even the dogs
But give me a fiddle and lord knows
I'd throw down
With the best of them.
One cart over from Pierre Falcon
On our way to Turtle Mountain

Party on the Prairies, Part II

My Uncle Dan puts the call out sometime in the Spring,
"We're going canoeing who's in?"
We've all been dreaming of following rivers, 4 pound
pickerel fillets, watching sunset loon air shows, clearing
campsites and trails that haven't been used since the
last time we passed through.
We email chain back and forth, bets are made, fights start,
a song request list circulates, and a route is planned.

Meet up with the Buffalo Pound boys at Bugsy's bar in PA,
Two Métis crews coming together in half ton Dodge's.
My Calgary cousin orders side avocado for his salad
And the server looks at him like he's gone insane,
"Noone's ever ordered that here before," she says.
We watch the chef sprint out of the back kitchen
Headed towards the Safeway.
He's got kids though so you gotta think of health you know.

The rest of us eat Big Boy Breakfast's
Slam plates down. Who's a big boy. I'm a big boy.
Texas Skillets, Clubhouse's, drink a couple cold beers.
Rehash stories from other canoe trips
Before the long drive north to Missinnipi.

My Uncle Dan doesn't believe in tie down straps,
Because there's nothing like stopping every half hour,
On a 12 hour drive, to check the ropes tying the canoes
Down to the trailer.
We lost a canoe once. It sailed up into the wind and landed
Right side up in a little lake off the side of the #2 highway.
Not a scratch on it.

We never see anyone in the North. Maybe a few fishing guides
Outside of the lodges. No other canoers (canoeists?). No other
People tripping through, because they can no longer follow
The bison or work the trade routes heading back to Portage.

My Uncle Dan,
Born two hundred years too late.
Would have been the ultimate 18th ce Métis man.
Living out on the prairies under the laws of the Cree matriarchs.
The guy wanders foothills, rivers, wherever he can,
Solo canoed the length of the Bow, South Sask, and Red Deer.
He would have been too independent for the HBC though
Would have went Pierre Grey style.
Cause you know, fuck corporations.

My Uncle Dan,
Taught me to respect relationships with everything.
Bring your sacred offerings.
We're lucky that the land
And the water, the birds, fish and animals, let us pass
Through here. Make sure to find the places that you need.
Give something back. Keep that with you wherever you go.
Tobacco down.

The Connor McDavid of Saskatoon Berries

They know you haven't been living out their
Windswept dreams
That the children's children might not starve.

But instead of starving off of food my generation
Starved knowing
We were disconnected from your voices, stories,
Poems, language, land.

And the way that you waded through the Flats off
Of Buffalo Pound Lake, picked wild mint, and peeled
Back the roots to give me a piece of gum, the way
Your Granny had done for you.
And the way that you could shake down a
Saskatoon bush,
Leaving no berry behind, was like watching an NHL
Player skate. You moved with such precision that even
The woodpeckers stopped their incessant
Pah
Pah
Pah
Pah
To watch the Métis version of Connor McDavid
Stickhandle Saskatoon berries into a 4L ice cream pail.

voyage

Toronto, Part I

Cities make me feel seven years old

Remembering how

Moose Jaw stretches on forever
And Regina is unfathomable in it's vast
Avenues and streets and towers
Red Lobster treasure chest.

I still get bewildered by the infinite lights
Fire working off of downtown Edmonton
Stretching to the southside across the river.

I've been here forever

When we were seventeen we walked
Endless along the banks staring up at
The possibility of night skies embedded in
Every hope, dream, and desire.

When you told me you were moving to Toronto
In an off hand Instagram message.
You had already been living in the sky for years.
Long separated from the prairie of Saskatchewan
With a business degree and an understanding of
Money. A bank account to reflect the
Fourteen hour days you work. We were
Always destined to live on other sides of the
Towers. Sky scraping. I can only imagine the way
Toronto light would reflect off your autumn
Hair in the early mornings fifty stories up.

I pulled up google maps and searched out the areas
That you live, breathe, work, eat, love in.
And wikipediaed their histories and stories. When
People were working in skyscrapers there, going to
Universities, drinking cocktails. The west was still
Under the laws of our Aunties and Grandmothers.
And would be for another hundred years.

I read comics and books about Toronto.
Wonder how you walk within crowds.

I paddle people up and down the river,
Play cards, hunt birds, train dogs, tell stories.
Doing what my family has been doing forever
Under the shadows of new prairie sky scrapers.
Instead of bison.

Toronto, Part II

You came back one summer,
In a flurry from Toronto, sent me an instagram message.
I need a break.

I picked you and your friend up from the Edmonton International in a 600,000 km Toyota 4Runner, that had seen more Rez road than pavement. And we bumped all the way out to the mountains. Wall tent trailer in tow and two Labrador retrievers in the back. Niska and Sisip.

You both wore muted tone extreme hiking clothes. Branded and I assumed flammable. Told me stories of your experiences working as two young, beautiful, women, Bay street. Not that I could comprehend how smart your world is or the words that you were saying.

I stayed away from money. Not that I wouldn't take a bump in the bank account, but I'd just have to give it to someone.

Your friend went to Columbia, BComm, MBA, grew up in New Jersey, had never seen a real Rocky Mountain. Or the glacial blue of the lakes and rivers. Or wild horses, sheep, and a big ol' fat bull moose that winked at me as we drove by. I told her about the history of the horse, and how the niitsitapi women I work with told me about their collective memory of horses that went away for a bit and then came back.

We talked about Métis settlements, and how Jasper is built on the bones and homes of Métis and Cree families. I assume there's a connection of sorts back to the money of Toronto and Montreal but I can't figure it out.

These were stories from the years after our undergrads when you were convinced that catching a fish was going to take away all the offhand comments from the shitheads you were working with. I wanted to beat the fuck out of them, because I don't know any better, and resorting to primal rage feels fucking good sometimes. But you said that I would end up in jail and that would just break me, like it's broken so many of your cousins, and friends. They're the type of guys that will have their dad's lawyer dialed up before you even swing the first punch.

And then what would you do with your dogs. So I took your advice and watched the light in your eyes fade.

In the sunset, I set up the wall tent while the two of you ran up the side of a mountain. The dogs circled around you, looking for ptarmigan and grouse. I built a big fire, threw some bulgogi marinated moose steaks on the grill, took pulls from a flask filled with Jameson and stared up the mountainside and watched as your headlamps turned on, one after the other. Two lights In the infinite darknes.

Loonie

This is a poem about a Loon. But it's not really about a Loon. It's about a girl. Hidden metaphors and shit. But I'm sure you already guessed where that was going. I may have spent too long up here in the North guiding tourists from Calgary/Texas who want an authentic river man, Métis fiddler, voyageur story teller, bear wrestler.

I can play the part perfectly, and I think I've spent too many fireside nights thinking about how I could play myself into your lifestyle of travelling across the continent from Vancouver to Toronto, weekly. I mean I've been from Buffalo Narrows to Nipawin? Same thing?

You make sales, or deals, or attend meetings, maybe all of the above. I'm not quite sure how it all works but it sounds important and your ability to command attention in any room you walk into makes me think of a mama Bear who will beat the shit out of anyone who tries to play you.

Chance encounters, like two Loons passing in the night, that I would meet you sitting at the Sheraton Cavalier, Saskatoon. You had been stranded from making it back to Toronto by another prairie blizzard that smashed flight schedules.

The university had brought me in to speak about teaching little ones the art of long distance bush canoeing. They never paid me anything, but gave me a swanky free room, and the time to visit my cousins. You said "those fuckers are taking advantage of you," but I didn't mind.

I tried to buy you a drink, but you pushed my scrap cash aside and said the "company can cover tonight. So this one is on me." I couldn't comprehend the depth of the cities you live in or the people you know. Just as I'm sure you can't imagine that I grew up in a house without running water or a phone in the 1990's.

I imagine that when I get off this river you'll be flying somewhere over the criss cross prairie grid, or shield lakes, or Rocky's. The mountains tend to do a better job of hiding the land's pain. If you've ever seen a Loon fly you know that it's not graceful. But it doesn't give a shit because it knows that it's the most famous bird in this thing called Canada.

Cry Havoc and Paint Blue the Crack of Night

We sat on a set of stairs in the Kingsway Mall parkade
And watched the thunderstorms paint the downtown sky
Scrapers dark metallic blue.

You told me that every building reminded you of a little city
From the Star Trek DVD's your cousins watched on endless
Loops back at Kohkum's.

We cracked cans of lucky lager straight out of a salmon pack.
And felt the dark rolling in over the city lights. We tried to
Paint our future in the shadows.

I smoked scholarship Canadian Classics and told you that
Someday I would take you back to Buffalo Pound and show
You the cabin I grew up in.

We talked about how we were going to make things better. But
We didn't know what better meant. To us that was security and
The chance to survive.

You told me that you'd change the world through your art.
You we're going to paint the city a thousand years in the
Past. Bring home the bison and the otters.

We were at the age where anything is possible, high school
Hadn't destroyed us the way they intended it to and
University had yet to make a dent in our future.

I marvelled in the way the dark blue metallic storm light
Turned your sheet straight hair into the iridescence of a raven.
You laughed and said you were related.

We had no idea that in three years I'd be bald and you'd be
Dead. Done and gone. Finito. Nothing is infinite, except the
Rivers and the storms and that's okay.

You were still too young though. And I miss you everyday.
Even if the last year we grew apart as I followed my path
Back through rehab and you burned down the University.

We couldn't put the words together on that night.
We just sat in the shelter of concrete and watched lightning
Pass through the flickering glow of the McDonald's
Golden Arches.

I should have wrapped you up in my words instead of my
Hoodie. An attempt to bring the dancing grouse in my
Stomach to a stop. An attempt to let you know just how
Beautiful you are.

I Dream of Bomb Ass Rivers (North Saskatchewan)

You're a goddamn prairie dragon
Rattlesnaking through my bison dreams
Ignoring Treaty and Territory borders
In an endless course to carry blood
And bones to the forever waters.

I heard a story once that a bison calf
Red as the sunrise, threw itself into
Your waters because it dreamed of
Montreal and the street of St. Laurent.

They tried to contain your rage with
Bighorn and Brazeau Dams
Flooding homeland and hunting territory
To placate your unchainable torrents.

I sat outside the old grave markers on
Your banks in the middle of the city and
Tried to skip rocks to the other side.
Wondering where the exact spot my
Grandmother's grandmother was born
And if they threw the placenta into the
Currents to let our relations know that you
Had come into this world.

Infinite Lek

In the haunted hills south of Moose Jaw
There's an infinite lek close to where my
Grandfather's ashes rest beside the bones
Of beloved Labrador's wrapped in their
Granny made Blankets. On the right spring
Day the lek will be filled with Sharptail Grouse
Dancing it out, waves of wings and tail feathers
Strong in the air as voices whisper off of
Old Wives lake. I wonder how much blood they
Step on with each practiced, careful move.
How long they have sat solo through long winters
Dreaming of the day they'll return to the lek,
And start prairie two stepping. Again.
I want to see a Sage Grouse, Prairie Bomber,
B52 flying out of the air force base to drop seeds
From her crop across Palliser's triangle of
Unlivable desolate desert prairie that no self
Respecting mooniyaw would ever move too.
But Palliser's prognosis didn't stop my matriarchal
Ancestors from living alongside the leks forever past.
They'll return one day just like the Sage Grouse
Will. They have to. I don't have much else.
In the way of dreams except to see those wings
Stretched out across the sun, catching the voices
Singing now, off of Old Wives lake and pulling up
And up and up over herds of millions of bison trailed
By wolves and grizzlies and coyotes and Nehiyawak
Métis, Sioux, Niitsitapi. Dancing across the prairie on
Their own leks that may have gone away for a bit but
They'll be back.

What Kind of Name is Hat for a Lake

Right off the entrance to Elk Island National Park
I saw a big bull moose, chilling out in a slough,
Lift his head to acknowledge us as we passed
By in the Toyota 4Runner. All rust. I wanted to
Tell you about the moose and how his antlers
Shone lightning in the sun's reflection off of the
Slough. How I wanted to catch that reflection and
Bottle it up, to try and regain some sense of the
Land taking us back. And throw the bottle up into
The depth of the sky, watch as it came back down
To Earth and shattered into the blood soaked soil.

We launched the canoe in Astotin. I made a joke about
Being bald and wearing hats, that you shrugged off.
Because I have a handsome head and you claim
To like the way it feels, scratching into your breasts
During the night. You wondered how much weight I
Would lose when I went back into the northern rivers.
And I thought it would probably just be you. Not that
I wanted this to end but 3 weeks apart in the heat of
The summers sheet lightning will move anyone into
Bed. But until then, I paddled you around the lake as
You dipped your hands, then your feet, then your hair
Into the water, reclaimed to the birds swooping us that
You were baptized in the blood of deceased rivers and
Lakes. The veins of our entangled existence. I'd paddle
You around under any sky.

Elephants

He smashes back two lines of coke
Walks into the 7-11 and threatens
To blow the heads off of the two
Working the night shift. For a couple
Packs of darts and tit mags. Relics of time.
Across the way in the parking lot of the McDonald's
She smokes a big bomber and sits back
Ready to order a couple cheeseburgers
Medium fries, big ass coke a cola.
Hell she makes a ketchup packet smear look sexy.

She smokes joints, writes undergrad papers
For straight cash, fucks, and serves drink.
Sometimes she fucks the undergrads she
Writes papers for and drinks their drinks and
Smokes their joints. Sometimes she doesn't.
He smashes back sugar packets in the tarped
Out traffic circle. Hidden from the commuters
Spinning circles around his head. He remembers
Wearing a neck tie and someone telling him
That he looks like an elephant and strung it up and hung.

Light the Bridge

Fresh out of sunny disposition
I stretch out to the sky seeking
    The
           Voices
                    Of
Everyone I know who has hung
Forever from extension chords
In unfinished concrete rental
housing basements.

They stare back at me on all the
Long drives home from late night
Degenerate behaviour. Card games
And such. I try to ignore their faces,
Suck in and hold my breath around
The dark side streets, alley entrances.

Lift your legs when you go over the
Train tracks.

Lift your legs when you canoe under
A bridge.

They can still hear your footsteps.

Abandoned Southside

Long before government jobs and teaching gigs put
Cash in my pocket, I walked from southside university
Parties back to 118th on any given night. Because I
Never had money for a cab or a pack of smokes and
The trains and buses stop at midnight. It gave me time
To drop beer caps, and cigarette butts off of the bridge
And watch them fall infinite towards black ice.

I could have left the party early, but I've never been one to
Miss an opportunity for an adventure, or conversation
With the women who tune me the fuck up in lecture hall
On Canadian History without the Indian that I have no
Reason to be part of. And who else in their twenties is
Going to shoot stolen fireworks off in the backyard in
Some weird attempt to get the smart women to notice him
Elementary school style. They sparkle, bubble, burn into
The trace light, city night, sky. I tried to see them come down.

And wouldn't it be something if I could get out of my own
Head enough to confide in the magpies that perch outside
The classrooms that make me feel so inadequate and just
Fucking small.

But I was a sucker for the idea that my alcoholic redemption
Would come in the form of words or wisdom from the people
Who never existed in any rural world I knew. And the city
Lights from the downtown skyline lit up my dreams, that
Anything is possible outside the confines of small town,
Anywhere, Canada.

Because I didn't know yet that being Métis is creating
Your own narrative around the history of your walks.
That under the bridge, the campfires of your Granny's
Family still burn, if you shut up you can still hear them
Singing long into the night, travelling songs, distinctive
Rhythms, that make a motherfucker want to get up and
Dance the long blocks back to the drudgy ass basement
Apartment behind the giant baseball bat.

A Brief History of My Childhood Injuries

Outside the abandoned southside hospital in Moose Jaw, SK
My friend Justin put the barrel of his single shot, pellet gun,
Pistol against my cheek and pulled the trigger. The pellet
Went through one cheek but didn't penetrate the other or
Break any teeth. And I've never felt so cold as I heard his
Footsteps, running. Running, while I tried to push the pellet
With my tongue into the hole to clog the blood slipping into
My mouth.

Snaring gophers in the yellow elementary school field
Because we couldn't get the hose all the way there
From the school and the janitor would pay us in 5 cent
Candy for each gopher we brought back to him dead
I snared one that didn't die and it chomped down on my
Finger like the sour soother I had in my mind
The doctors decided that rabies shots were in order
To be safe, 2 in the butt, 12 in the gut, 2 in the shoulder
For weeks and weeks and weeks. But my world has a
Place for kids immune to rabies and I became the first
Call with my broom when a raccoon had found its way
Into a place it wasn't supposed to be. Skunks too.

Playing road hockey a neighborhood kid took his stick
And smashed me over the head with it for reasons that
Are still vague to me, but I woke up in a pile of blood
With the other kids around me and someone's mom
Screaming and loading me into her old Ford Windstar
That reeked of VLT's and stale McDonald's burgers.
Doctor mangled the stitches and I have a beautiful
Scar and head wounds always look worse than they
Actually are. And I heard that the same guy who shot
Me in the cheek beat the fuck out of the kid at school.

Eating Macaroni Soup

When I was out "social working"
I missed the idea of writing poems
But I thought about them lots when I was:
Hunting Moose
Hunting Grouse
Eating Macaroni Soup and Baloney Sandwiches
Talking to women who deserve to be the subjects of poems
And not obituaries
Talking to children who will unfortunately be the subject
Of government statistics
Talking to politicians who will use the obituaries and
Statistics to get elected
Listening as media outlets continually overlook the good
Work being done
So they can get to the crimes and drugs and gangs
    That didn't exist in my world.
    But somehow exists in theirs.
Listening to the stories of our ancestors. The real stories.
Not the media ones.

Directions to the Culture Grounds

Social Worker Version
(as recited through the telephone and then sent in an email for confirmation)

Drive west on the Whitemud
Keep going when it turns into Hwy 628
Turn left on Winterburn Road
Turn right on Lapotac Blvd
Follow the old tipis in

They can't make it though, busy doing paperwork

Elder Version
(as recited through the telephone, no email confirmation)

Head straight out past the city heading west until you hit the edge of the reservation. Turn left and go down until you see the old sand hills on the right hand side of the road, just past Dave's old trailer. Watch out for RCMP; they're always out. Drive past the Cardinal sign on the left hand side of the road. They haven't thrown any water down in a few years and the dust has really been kicking up so watch out for dogs. Go past my Nokhums shack, where I was raised. Turn left at that old lodge. The one hidden in the trees. Follow the ruts down the trail, unless the boys have brought gravel and filled them in. In that case, follow the gravel. Either way follow the trail back into the birch trees past the family of prairie chickens crushing gravel into their gizzards. Don't shoot any, those are my chickens. You leave those chickens alone. Go past the gate, you might have to move it. It's dummy locked and it will swing once you work the rust out of the hinge. Hasn't swung well for about 10 years. So you'll need to give it a good pull for encouragement. On the right side you'll see faded yellow, red, and white prints hanging in the trees. Those are from our family my boy. Though you may have never met them they put those there for you. If you can hear the magpies squawking your arrival you'll be at the right place. You'll see the old sundance lodges where the boss tree still stands strong even though everything else has gone back to the land. There's a little shack with a tin roof surrounded by piles of those good lava rocks, the ones from Clearwater, and river rocks, and rocks that have cracked. Some old green and blue tarps, getting pretty holy so we've doubled them up on the chopped birch. Don't look at that green cut birch, it still needs to find its place. Another shack, this one circular with a rusted out stove pipe coming out the roof will be farther back past the next strand of birch and willow trees and the grass field. Hopefully the boys have cut that grass by now, was getting pretty long. There should be smoke coming out of that chimney. Come inside, we'll be waiting for you.

Maverick

Somewhere out east the sun's rising
It's stretching out over the trees horror frost
Running shadows up the cutline

We're sitting on two stumps
Watching the line with nervous conviction of a
Google maps choice
180 grains chambered, safeties off

Mutual appreciation for silence
Maverick nods at me then raises his rifle and scopes the bush
Stops and points barrel down

A stud buck four by four
Walks out of the bush and grazes on the cutline,
Shoulder view
Sights him in at 150 yards

I'm waiting for the squeeze
The inevitable drop head pounding shattered
Snow stained red

The buck stares at us, flannels and jeans.
Then he's gone and the cutline sits without ghosts
My friend lowers his rifle

We wait without words
For another hour until the steady popcorn popping firearms
Send us back to the truck

Turn on Indian radio, we drink
Premixed baileys and McDonalds black
Styrofoam cups and wheat kings

House Fire

A murder of crows moved into the tall jack pine in the backyard of the block's meth house. Thousands of black wings holding court. Just outside the reach of the pinted out people's rocks. They condemn them for their sins of gluttony, greed, lust and having a good time. Before they adjourn and take wing to go and rip open the alley's trash bags, pulling out old chicken wing bones to scatter across the block like little beating hearts.

One of them spray painted, *here be methys*, on the decaying garage door. Black paint scrawled over chipped green in crow scratch to announce the verdict passed down from the highest branches of the big ass jack pine. Crows write in cursive exclusively.

The methys, as the crows call them, steal an old daisy BB gun to plink the crows out of the trees. They pump air into the daisy with the vigor of an eighth grade handjob, pull the trigger, and release the bb's with all the acclaim of a dribbled cum shot that falls far short of its expectation.

Failing to fuck them up. The methys torch the tall, big ass, dried out jack pine. And the wood snaps alive under the flames. It's gone in an instant. The fire takes out everything. House, garage, courthouse. The methy's flee and the crows caw away to their next trial. A bulldozer shows up and knocks down the charred out remnant followed by a couple of the methys looking for an old hit they left behind. One of them carries a bag of dill pickle spitz and he shoots seeds all over the lot. At the end of the summer there are thousands of sunflowers stretching yellow tall towards the sun.

TRC Combo

Like 10 years ago if you bought a
Jr. Chicken, Bacon Cheeseburger,
And a McDouble, the total came to
$4.20 but only in Saskatchewan,
Just the way tax works I guess.
My cousins and I would smash back
420 combos as we and every other
Crew of young dumb kids referred
To them, on our endless walks home
From bars. A McDonald's in Saskatoon
At 3 AM is a party when you're 21.
When you're 31 and you order a 420
Combo at 3 AM it's just sad. But I
Have to try and recapture my memories
Because they tend to be fleeting at
This point and I long for the way my
Brain felt when I was young and dumb
And didn't realize the drudgery of what
The "Aboriginal" government internship
Would bring. Or how it would just shatter
Any dream I ever had of making a deal
With the land.

Sweetgrass Dreams

Last night Wikaskokiseyin
Chief Sweetgrass
Showed up on the doorstep of my home in Hazeldean,
Papaschase IR 136
With my friends Jeremy and Jeff from Little Pine

The boys had snow shovels and a tiger torch
and told me they meant to bring Spring
They started clearing all the snow from my backyard
Just yelling and laughing in Cree
Like a bunch kehtestim

When they finished bringing Spring
They came up to the front door dripping sweat
Jeremy, on behalf of Chief Sweetgrass
(his English is as rough as my Cree)
Asked for newo sisipwak in exchange
For all their work

Sorry boys, I'm fresh out of ducks, I said.
I gave the last of them to an old man from Enoch
And oh, did they ever get mad
Chief Sweetgrass, Wikaskokiseyin
Learns English in a hurry and yells
Why doesn't anyone have any goddamn ducks.
And the three of them storm off bringing
Spring with every step

Fiddle Me Home

I spent enough time locked up
For the years lost
That's all I'm going to say about that

When I saw you playing the fiddle
In the school band
Snow & Wolves howled all around
Each year became slush turning to ice
Under thousands of trampling dancing feet
I slid along to the sounds of seventh
Grade scratching bows

Has it really been that long?
Has the ice ever melted?
Did you ever start playing so fast
That the feet got twitching stomping
The heat from the soles melting
And the wolves howling
And the years melting
Melting
Melting
Away

The Common

On those muggy summer nights we'd wade through the
Legislature Fountain And stare into the spotlights,
Illuminating the faux euro facade, Purple town we
Called it. Everything appeared purple. Even your body
When you stripped down and swam laps through the
Wading pool. While the street kids watched jaws so
Low they forgot to ask for cigarettes. The one time I forgot
To take off my jeans before you tackled me into the
Wading pool, a mess of curly hair and brown skin.
We decided to fuck pants and threw them off the
High Level Bridge. Two pairs of skinny jeans circling down
To the water. I wanted to light them on fire but you
Said that was juvenile as you crawled up for a piggyback
To your roommates after party. And you said something
About how we were never going to get old. I believed
You then as we drank Old Milwaukee's, smoked cigarettes
And watched the sun rise. We did our best to block out the
Bbio grad student who wouldn't shut up. Ironic that you
Would move to Vancouver with a carbon copy of that pylon.
Given how much shit you talked about him. How you
Believed that there was more out there. Every now and then
I check Instagram to see that old photo of you in bed a tussle
Of sheets and hair and the smile that told me that there was
No reason to stop believing now.

la keu di renn

It's All Magpies

It's all Magpies
Maybe write about an Eagle or something instead
It's been this way since 2010, when you finished
Grade 12 and started yelling at old balls professors,
Tagging up the 97th street pedestrian bridge with
A subtle, Quit Your Job. While secretly, desperately
Wishing that someone would hire you. Get off that
Value menu. Stop stealing books from the Chapters
Then reselling them at the used bookstore down the
Way for cigarette money and maybe a six pack.

It's all Magpies
Maybe write about a Raven or something instead
Then people will start taking your writing seriously
Big black foreboding omens scattered all throughout
High school/Undergrad English courses, and the
Garbage dumps of the north where they catch wind
That some shithead eighteen year old is carving a
Metaphor through emo chains into his crummy ass
Basement apartment wall. Hoping that one of the
Artsy women will notice that he's a writer and edgy
And not a broke ass little bitch that can't afford the
Diesel jeans and Lacoste shoes that make up undergrad
Lecture halls. He rides the giant baseball bat
While his friend, fresh out of rehab, pushes in circles.

It's all Magpies
Maybe write about a Owl or something instead
But those birds only sell death and the last time
One was heard one hooting it's way down 118th
Woke up to a Facebook message that a friend
Strung himself up and called it a day. But since
That seemed to happen all the time just shrugged

And put on stolen GAP sweater vests to try and
Be a middle class, suburb kid, and impress the
Smart ones from English class with how poetic
A sweater vest made me look.

It's all Magpies
Maybe write about something arbitrary and vague
Something that will make people sit down and think
They're smart because you use big words and turn
Thesaurus pages with the emphasis of a toaster ovens
Alarm. Or the thwack of an axe hitting the apartment door
A case of mistaken identity, they wanted the dealer one
Apartment building over. But if you don't even know what
A verb or a grammar is then how the hell are you going
To write something for graduate students to over analyze
And judge your insecurities.

It's all Magpies
Maybe write something about reconciliation or the TRC
White people love that shit. Makes them feel good.
And when they read your writing they'll think that you're
One of the good ones and that you're really getting this
Whole conformity thing and probably a government
Internship and some spots in the local media because
You're always willing to share a story, unpaid, of course
Because you can't get compensated and you're scared
That no one will care. Which they don't. But it's easier
To think that what you're doing is making a difference
Than to be told it doesn't.

A Magpie/Métis Boy Visits Tkaronto

I flew down Queen St. West to my friend's
Sausage bar. Nipping at people's nice leather.
I'm a squawking mess of iridescent Magpie
Feathers, blackgreen, whites and purples,
Wearing my fancy city clothes
Which means my stiffest plaid
Just potato-starch collars, so stiff.
And blue jeans that aren't covered
In pothole trash and McDonald's coffee cups.
And a fancy hat, with a nêhiyawi-napew
Wearing a headdress of woodpecker feathers
Muted brown, so no one in nice leather will say.

That's cultural appropriation you know.

I'd rather save my energy to
Kisôwe tahkiskâcikew pîkiskwewin
With the beautiful big city women
Who will be flocking to my friend's bar.
It's nice to be half Magpie/half Métis
You drink for free all over Tkaronto, Toronto.
And at a party later that night a beautiful
Big
City
Woman
In nice leather
Tells me,
I love this Alberta chic thing you got going on.

A Magpie/Métis Boy Visits A&W

It's nice to be half Magpie/half Métis
No one cares that I'm getting super fat
From my perch outside the A&W
Drive thru, just shoveling teen burgs
And greasy poutines into my beak
Not a big root beer guy and their coffee
Sucks butt.

The best time to be there is when the
Karaoke lounge across the avenue
Opens up its doors to release the smokers
And the sounds of ironic full-blood Métis
Tapping out spoons and fiddles to
Whiskey before the dawn.
Joking, Céline Dion.
Greets me from my perch and I can
Mow down these burgers with the
Noise music of my cousins cascading
Over my beady black eyes, hallow eyes.
Crescent moon eyes.
Teen burger in talon.
I hop a little jig, smash the burger grease
Into the pavement, where it seeps through
The cracks to rest next to my ancestors'
Blood and bones.

A Magpie/Métis Boy Finds Some Moose Bones

It's nice to be half Magpie/half Métis
Dipping wings across the shadows of
Skyscrapers. Buildings of hot trash just
Waiting to find its way to the streets, alleys
Backs of rusted-out Toyotas. Sleds of Moose bones
Wait for me to call my cousins to feast on
The frozen red meat still clinging to the
Bones. We can't carry them on our backs
The way I can out of the bush when I'm not
The magpie or the coyote. Just a half-breed
Walking for whatever a mile is. Plus twenty.
Towing a sled of moose bones for my magpie
Cousins to come and have their feast.
For the purple-green flash of wings and
Startled white fronts stained red with Moose
And the hot trash of a city. Moose bone blood
Looks different than McDonald's ketchup.
While I nibble, I hope that the moose bones will
Rise up to become a two-year-old bull. Tall as all hell.
Snorting and stomping hot-breath thermals that carry
My wings high above the city.

A Magpie/Métis Boy Attends Ukrainian Christmas

It's nice to be half Magpie/half Métis
Except on Ukrainian Christmas when
I'm neither.
That night I'm all diborsha and wheat under
Placemats, pierogies, and those round crêpe-
Wrapped sourdough thingies with dill in them.
Cheers and fiddle music. And fancy flower shawls.
I say funny words in Cree that sound like funny words
In Ukrainian and my grandfather tells stories of
Setting up pins in a bowling alley in Sheho, Saskatchewan.
Before he spoke English, before his brother
Bought the bar. And the farms went under.
I'm a scavenger by birthright. Hauling barbwire across
Prairie fields. Picking at the dust of red-river carts.
Finding Pemmican balls in parfleche bags but
They're rock hard and my beak can't smash into them.
The way I want it too.
Magpies aren't Ukrainian. Métis people can be.

A Magpie/Métis Boy Fights a Blue Jay

It's nice to be half Magpie/half Métis
Except when you travel out to Tkaronto, Toronto
To attend a Blue Jays game
I forgot that I'm supposed to fight Blue Jays on sight
It's embedded in my magpie DNA
But my grandmother who's ¾ Métis ¼ bushpie
Loooooves the Blue Jays
But only the 2002 version
She hasn't known a player since.
My Blue-Jay-loving grandmother drinking whiskey
By herself in an apartment on the northside
Betrayed me. She must have told the Blue Jays
That I was coming to the city, because oh they,
Oh they, oh they, were ready.
I could barely gulp down my foot-long hotdog
And big beer. Before they came in with that Caaawaaakkk
Caaaawaaaakkkk, cawaaakkkk, striiiiiiikkkeeeee
Raining foul balls down on my seat,
But really just playing like shit.
They lost 8-0 to the Cleveland Indians
And I didn't make any new friends.

A Magpie/Métis Boy Watches Some Cranes

It's nice to be half Magpie/half Métis,
I have an appreciation for how high
Cranes fly over this city skyscrapers
That jut out like the blackened stumps
Of a forest fire. Perched on my deck
Pecking away at the discarded bones
Of a Domino's thiccc crust pepperoni
Pizza. I listen to the Cranes passing
Through the city night, where concrete
Presses down on the tears and blood
Of my Grandmother's relations it sends
Whispers of bison hunts, and songs,
And old stories, spiralling up between
The blackened stumps to catch the wings
Of the Cranes, propelling them north.

Magpies don't belong in the north.
That's raven country and I'm content
To cheer on the Cranes from my low perch
As they dream of the crisp, clear, shield lakes.
Bellies full of whatever it is that Cranes
Eat but the red markings around their
Eyes tell me that it's something different
Than the fast food scraps that I plunge
My beak into. My Malamute cousin spent
A winter digging an internet line for Inuvik
And he talked about Cranes that towered
Over the tundra. Their legs as long as the
Tallest corporate headquarters. When they

Fly they drop feathers that shatter rivers into
The earth. Hungry Cranes would pick up the
Workers with their beaks, and flip them up
In the air Jurassic Park style for a snack.
The crew had to carry old Rez 30-30's, the
Gun that every museum has sitting in his truck.
Warped barrel and all, but the bullets just
Annoyed the Cranes, blackfly style.

A Magpie/Métis Boy Goes Golfing

It's nice to be half Magpie/half Métis
The gods of gutter life, anything that hits the streets
Belongs to me and my cuzzins. It's our reconciliation
Bitches. I'm into shine, sparkle and getting my beak
All slimed up with the grease from the 3 AM pizza
Crusts. It's a style. So suck on that you woodpecker
Fuck, thinking you're so cool with your fancy ass red
Tufts and beak tuned with the pa pa pa pa's you peck
Around. Woodpecker's remind me of the people who
Golf on private courses. Me and my cousins are public
All day. But I dream of carrying that infinite burning stick
And torching all the fairways, open up the nesting grounds
Maybe the other birds and bison would come back if
They had prairie grass again. Then we wouldn't have to put
Up with the incessant pa pa pa pa pa pa. That's all I hear.
I want to take my driver and smash a tee shot with prairie
Winds and carry it all the way to Montreal with a little note
Written in the dimples, my mutt DNA.

A Magpie/Métis Boy Gets a Government Job

It's nice to be half Magpie/half Métis
Opened up a can of government jobs and internships
All at the bottom of the rung of course, my voice doesn't
Matter. And why the fuck is everything so white. It's so
White you can hear those fluorescent lights humming
Along. Just too quiet, and the cubicles, and the chatter
Of keyboards typing, and the headphones, and the nabob,
And the salary, and the catered lunches. I like the catered
Lunches, I sneak out the leftover crusted sandwiches tuna,
And veggie and maybe the weird roast beef and the chickpea,
A half Magpie/half Métis boy can't be picky. I don't think it's
Office etiquette to stuff my beak with everything in sight.
Or to mention that they're not really doing a good job of
Integrating culture into their policy. But shit, that's a white
Problem not mine. They'll always find a way to take my
Sisters and brothers, cousins, mothers, no matter what I do.
So I may as well take my bomb ass 52k a year and go sit down
On the legislature grounds and read *Game of Thrones*.
Wishing that the dragons torched the legislature like my
Family used to torch the fort.

A Magpie/Métis Boy Goes Out on the Trapline

It's nice to be half Magpie/half Métis
My friend lets me go out on his trapline with him
We wander the back alleys of the old Papaschase IR 136
Checking the traps that he's set for bottles/cans/bikes
The good shit that brings in more money than my
Grandfather ever did. He uses an old purple bike attached
To a beat up kid trailer to make the rounds fast.
Replaced the dog sled and then the snowmobile
With that shit. Silent deadly. We pounce on the traps
Make sure that no one is rabid in the busted up concrete.
He pokes tiny holes in the blue recycling bags and
Carefully removes the cans make sure that no one is
Leaving a mess, it goes against all my instincts.
I want to grab that recycling bag and rip it into shreds
And toss the garbage all over the alley and pick out the
Crumbs of Domino's cardboard boxes. UNI discounted.
My friend says that will bring the heat on us and
His trapline will get shut down. The animals will go away.
They've done it before. They can do it again you know.

We've replaced conibears with student housing.
We've wrapped baled our fur in bags hauled
Hours to the trading post for 5 cents to the can.
Papaschase IR 136 was never supposed to
Produce anything for us. But we've managed
To strut our survival over cracked asphalt
Dodging city wolves with their howling sirens.
Intent on eating us alive.

Acknowledgments

I would like to thank everyone in my family, especially Pat, Ron, Kathleen and Peter. Marilyn Dumont, Ruth DyckFederhau and Norma Dunning for being constant supporters since my baby undergrad days. UBC Creative Writing Department. Bob Cardinal, George Desjarlais, Joe Ground, Rocky Morin, Kristin "Kokhum" Miller, Jeremy Albert, Delores Cardinal, Wilson Bearhead, Alvena Strasbourg, and countless others for all the teachings over the years. Emily Riddle for the constant writing tuneups. The staff and students at NorQuest Indigenous Student Centre and MacEwan University kihew waciston. And of course Marguerite Prodor, Niska, Nama, and Zaya for ensuring that I keep following birds and dreams.

www.ingramcontent.com/pod-product-compliance
Lightning Source LLC
Chambersburg PA
CBHW020915080526
44589CB00011B/604